so you want to join Mountain Rescue?

Mountain Rescue Explained

DAVID ALLAN & JUDY WHITESIDE

HAYLOFT

C000016518

First published 2006
Hayloft Publishing Ltd., Kirkby Stephen, Cumbria, CA17 4DJ

telephone: +44 (0) 17683 42300
fax: +44 (0) 17683 41568
email: books@hayloft.org.uk
web: www.hayloft.org.uk

copyright © David Allan FRCS
© Judy Whiteside
ISBN 1 904524 478

A catalogue record for this book is available from the British Library.

This book is sold subject to the condition that it shall not, by way of trade or otherwise, be lent, re-sold, hired out or otherwise circulated in any form of binding or cover other than that which it is published and without a similar condition including this condition being imposed on the subsequent purchaser.

Cartoons by David Allan.
Artwork by Judy Whiteside.
Excerpts from *Mountain Rescue* by Bob Sharp and Judy Whiteside
used with kind permission.

Printed and bound in the EU.

Papers used by Hayloft are natural, recyclable products made from wood grown in sustainable forests. The manufacturing processes conform to the environmental regulations of the country of origin.

contents

introduction

I have been involved with mountain rescue in a number of roles for a little over thirty years. During that time I have come to respect the people who provide the service for their commitment, their skills, and their capacity to endure. However, I have also come to believe that perhaps the most essential requirement for a successful mountain rescue team member is a sense of humour and it is in recognition of this that this book is produced.

I must pay tribute to the excellent book *Mountain Rescue* by Bob Sharp and Judy Whiteside which I have parodied and used as a source of ideas.

David Allan

A percentage of profits from sale of this book will go to mountain rescue

The way we were...

'...before the eighteenth century, hill walking and climbing for pleasure were virtually unknown. Life was hard enough without expending further energy pursuing the dubious pleasures of a cold, steep unforgiving landscape.'

'The team in the next valley have a thing called a stretcher...'

'Following a series of accidents, the climbing world began to consider the idea of developing a stretcher specially adapted for mountainous terrain...'

'This new issue cas-carrier thingummyjig don't 'alf take the strain off yer 'ips.'

'And when it all went wrong, the only people around to rescue you (if you were very, very lucky) were your mates, armed with nothing more than a five barred gate, a bit of rope and young men's belief that they were invincible, even if you apparently weren't!'

'We'll 'ave it back before dark, mister. Honest.'

There are many reasons why people join...

'The most amazing thing about a mountain rescue call out is the complete transformation of priorities it causes. Everything is dropped. Meals are left uneaten. Friends are left without a host. Long planned outings are postponed.'

'Don't wait up.
Love you... xxx'

'...every call out is an adventure, a challenge, each situation a test of ability, the satisfaction of working together as a team, the ever so slight frisson of being on the hill at a time you wouldn't normally ever dream of (late at night, pitch black, disgusting weather conditions...'

'Mountain rescue – on call 24/7. Rain or shine.'

'Another team member admitted that mountain rescue had awakened a deep interest in first aid...'

'...it goes without saying team members must have a caring nature and wish to help those in distress.'

'...what about motivation? A better word might be attitude. Mountain rescuers have it in bucket loads...'

'So that's settled then. You're having a baby and I'm joining mountain rescue...'

'When his bleeper goes off, it always seems to be at an inopportune moment.'

'You do know that last piece doesn't match, don't you?'

'According to the dictionary, to volunteer is to spontaneously undertake a task. The thing about mountain rescue is that spontaneity isn't really the name of the game. Spontaneity implies individual activity on the spur of the moment, rather than the carefully considered teamwork actually involved. Yet look up the word spontaneous and, several semi colons down the page you find *instinctive, automatic* and, more to the point, *prompted by no motive*. And there we have it...

'...mountain rescue team members, in general, appear to do what they do because they enjoy it. That's it.'

So you want to join?

'Occasionally, people talk their way into a team on false pretences, or without a clear understanding of what might be asked of them.'

Team members must be competent mountaineers in all weather conditions...

'There will usually be a set of critical requirements such as fitness or special skills which have to be met. Individuals who meet the criteria, sometimes established through an interview or questionnaire, will join as trainees or probationers.'

'There's no need to be nervous, young man... just a couple of informal questions and then we can all go home.'

Training will be provided...

'Teams practice and develop the kinds of skills you'd expect – first aid, casualty handling, radio communications, security on steep ground, avalanche awareness, pyrotechnics, searching, working with helicopters, incident management and so on.'

Soon you will learn the essential knots...

'Teams typically set up annual training programmes, meeting on a regular basis across the year, either on outdoor exercises – getting to know their own terrain and the nature and range of incidents they are likely to meet...'

...and good navigational skills are essential.

...or indoors, in the form of lectures and demonstrations.'

'...you should all by now be familiar with the two perfect mounds right in the heart of our patch.'

'We've always tried the flares outside the base before today.'

'Team members support one another, work in small groups and look to the safety of each other. When they find themselves dangling at the end of a rope or balanced on steep exposed ground, safety systems ensure that high risk procedures are fail safe.'

'Y'know... I always imagined this steep ground stuff might be a bit more technical...'

'That said, there are occasions when the elements do their best to conspire against even the best laid plans. It is precisely at those moments when the rigorous training instilled into team members – combined with the basic human instinct to survive – comes into its own.'

'Frankly, this is not what I expected a winter practice to be!'

'Nature may hold a good many of the cards, but the training practices and distillation of experience – sometimes measured in hundreds of years – which are central to every rescue team are surely the aces up their collective sleeves?'

Training is usually carried out 'in house' using the skills and knowledge of the more experienced team members...

'The view that mountain rescuers drink copious amounts of alcohol at every opportunity is not a myth we are able to dispel!'

'Okay chaps. A couple more boxes to tick then we can all get down to the pub... er, guys?'

Your team leader will
carry out appraisals.

'There they stood, windswept and masculine, exchanging whatever signals mountain rescue people do when they meet on the hill – establishing provenance; wise words about the weather; assumed nonchalance.'

'Yesterday? The course finished yesterday?!'

You will learn some new terms...

Running belay: A device attached to a rock face through which a climbing rope runs freely, acting as a pulley if the climber falls.

Hanging belay:
A generally uncomfortable belay stance on steep rock where there is no place to stand.

Synchronised line search: Observation by each person has to be structured and disciplined – looking to the front, left, right, behind, underneath, over the top – and bearing in mind that attention can wander very easily.

Mobile One: Probably the most expensive piece of equipment a team is likely to own... of which all team members will take very great care.

Last Known Position:
Indicates that the person
was not actually seen,
but that some item,
identified as theirs, has
been found.

You will become familiar with the equipment...

'Mountain rescue team members are on call through the 999 system, 24 hours a days, 365 days a year. They are as likely to leave a warm bed in the wee small hours to rescue an injured climber on some blizzard blown crag, as hunt the grounds of your local nursing home in search of someone's missing granny.'

'If you have fallen, Press 1. If you are lost, Press 2...'

Oxygen and Entonox are used regularly by teams to great effect. Vital though both these gases are, the sheer weight of the heavy steel bottles put them way down the popularity stakes when it comes to team members carrying kit up the hill.'

In recent years, many teams have been able to switch to lightweight aluminium cylinders...

'The vac matt is basically a flat, airtight beanbag on which the casualty is laid before being wrapped up in it. Once the person is secure, the air inside the bag is pumped out, producing a semi-rigid cocoon in the shape of the casualty. This limits movement and provides a total body splint, which effectively reduces the worsening of any injuries already sustained.'

During use, it's common to expel some of the air initially to allow the mattress to be used as a semi-rigid working platform.

'Other special items include portable blood pressure monitors as well as programmed defibrillators for use in the treatment of heart attacks.'

'Dear Sir,
I decided to service our defibrillator...'

Stretchers provide stability and safety for the casualty and enable rescuers to carry an injured person across uneven terrain for long distances.

'The most commonly used Bell stretcher dismantles into two halves, allowing it to be carried by two people to the casualty site where it can be reassembled ready for immediate use.'

'Okay, Phil. Give me the other half of the stretcher...'

...and well versed in casualty care...

'The Mountain Rescue Council has established a course which leads to a national Casualty Care Certificate. Teams generally do their own training, following an agreed syllabus under the guidance of the team medical officer, at the end of which there is a written 'multiple choice question' test and a range of practical scenarios.

'Examinees must please remember to fill in their name and team details before handing in their test papers...'

It's all well and good having the right medical equipment but team members must also have the skills to match. All team members should be capable of CPR and basic life support involving ABC assessment – Airway, Breathing, Circulation – but it is by no means obligatory that they sit the exam.

Many team members prefer to stay on the sidelines in casualty care and there is no pressure on them to undertake the full course.

'The examiner's decision is final and team members are unable to re-sit an exam within a six month period.'

'Yes, well when I wrote that you had absolutely no aptitude for casualty care... what I meant...'

Team members often practice with the hypodermic needle, using each other as guinea pigs, prior to injecting a real casualty...

'The quantities of controlled drugs made available to teams, their storage and use, is strictly controlled and monitored. Only those team members who hold the MRC Casualty Care Certificate are permitted to administer morphine...'

'Scout around and see if you can find a dock leaf.'

Rescue teams use a
variety of special splints
to immobilise fractures
but they might also
employ a number of other
very simple procedures.

'...and only those team members with the full certificate are insured to treat casualties.'

'Sorry... my Cas Care Certificate ran out at midnight yesterday.'

'Mountain rescue teams have moved a long way from those early days of limited equipment...'

'Can you nip down to Woolworth's for a couple of batteries?'

'Team members generally are trained to recognise and provide first aid for a wide variety of problems..'

'There's nothing at all about this in the Cas Care Book...'

'...asthma, angina, heart attack, hypoglycaemia, anaphylaxis, epilepsy, near drowning, lightning injury, hypothermia...'

'I'm sorry... we don't appear to have a plaster.'

'Most accidents take place in remote locations so scoop and run isn't an option. In theory, the rescue team member first on scene at a traumatic accident must be sufficiently capable – and confident – in delivering not only immediate first aid treatment but, with the help of other team members, in making the casualty comfortable for what might be a prolonged stretcher carry off the hill.'

'...and to think I could be sat at home watching Casualty...'

...and finally, you will be on the call out list.

'I know he would move heaven and earth for his family. It's just when that bloody bleeper goes off – so does he...'

'I didn't sleep a wink – can't believe I made it onto the call out list!'

'It can put a strain on family life and domestic harmony at times, when the children need attention or need to be taken to parties or school...'

'Team members keep their kit at home to be immediately ready for a call out.'

'...yet when the bleeper goes off, I'm there to make up the sandwiches, fill the flask, make appropriate soothing noises and, once he's gone, wait uneasily for his return.'

Team members rely on the support of those on the other side of the bed when the call comes in the midst of sleep...

You will be expected to help with fund raising...

Methods of fund raising will vary from team to team...

'Over the years, many teams have established sponsorship deals with various companies and organisations wishing to be associated with mountain rescue. These arrangements tend to work in healthy symbiosis...'

'I'm not against sponsorship as such, but this is ridiculous!'

'In a climate of endemic charity fatigue, teams must take advantage of local resources and contacts to generate funds.'

'All I said was, 'Why don't we join forces with cave rescue on the fund raising front...'

'...there are sponsored walks, sponsored abseils from city centre tower blocks, sponsored tandem sky dives; endurance events, wine tastings, hot pot suppers, barbecues, spring fairs, Christmas fairs, kit sales and open days, safety covers, tin shakes and collection boxes; gift aid donations, legacies, tombolas and raffles...'

'On balance, I think I preferred the wine tasting idea...'

'...and every single penny raised is valued.'

'I think the equipment budget for next year just rolled under the desk...'

...and help maintain the team base.

'So I said to the missus...'

'We'll probably never know the real cost of running an efficient mountain rescue service because those involved give so much of their time, and put their hands in their pockets so frequently to fund their 'hobby', it's impossible to assess.'

'It costs money to train people, maintain and run vehicles and rescue posts...'

'Every ounce of value will be squeezed from every resource.'

'It keeps them occupied between call outs.'

'We are receiving reports that the opening of the new lakeside mountain rescuer base has been delayed...'

But why so few women in mountain rescue?

'Women make up barely 5% of teams. Some say it may be that a macho image puts off a lot of female would-be members. However, they are likely to receive an encouraging reception...'

New members will usually receive comprehensive vehicle orientation training from the more experienced team members...

'Women have been involved with mountain rescue for many years...'

'I've been telling the wife I'm on a call out and now she's joined the damned team!'

'Molly Porter, a founder member of the Cairngorm team in 1964, was probably the first female rescue team leader in the UK. Her colleagues at the time were in awe of the exceptional amount of time she invested in team affairs. Besides mountain rescue, she was a qualified mountain guide and took part in many mountaineering expeditions across the world, at one point gaining the interesting accolade of 'Britain's Highest Housewife' from *Woman's Own* magazine.'

'Fetches them up really white and so kind to my hands.'

'Women have been retaining their femininity on the mountain for over a century...'

'...and then cook on a low light for about one hour thirty minutes...'

And why so many dogs?

'If we're really being honest, in the world of mountain rescue, it is very often the dog who is the hero...

'Well, you can't really complain, sir... at least he found you!'

'It's the dog doing all the hard work and wearing a nifty little search and rescue number...'

'What d'you mean it's my turn to do some work for a change?'

'...it's the dog who is calling the shots on the hill, though their human handlers (and their two legged team mates) might beg to differ a little.'

'No, you cannot have a GPS and that is absolutely my final word on the matter.'

'Quite apart from their air-scenting abilities, the naturally companionable search and rescue collie will happily snaffle all your butties, pee on your boots and give you a generous face wash...'

'You're very kind but couldn't you just go and tell them where I am?'

'It has to be said that any dog can be trained provided the chemistry between dog and owner is right.'

'Okay. I'll ask you nicely. Please, pretty please, when you've got a minute, d'you think you could pop round that nice field over there and see if you can find anyone. There's a good chap.'

'It is well known that collies have an irrepressible tendency to round up almost anything that moves, including people and vehicles, sometimes to their cost.'

'...and you're not coming down until you apologise.'

'...learning ability, stamina and vitality are the key criteria for a good search dog.'

'Oh no...'

'The entire training process is one of encouragement. Human scent brings praise, whereas the indication of hares, deer or birds fails to impress.'

'That is not smart. It isn't clever. And it is definitely not funny.'

'Dogs are trained to indicate their find to their handler – usually by running back and forth between the two and barking loudly. Indeed, whichever way they can best attract their handler's attention.'

'Owoooooooooooooooogh!!!!!'

The training required of a dog and handler is very demanding and exceptionally time consuming, through a programme that extends to five grades. Many have fallen at the first hurdle. And failure can weigh heavily on the potential dog team.

'Wait... I'm sure we can take the assessment again...'

Then there are the helicopters...

'Whether winching or landing, the down-draught produced by a helicopter's rotor blades can easily knock a fifteen stone man off his feet...'

People, livestock and any loose equipment must always be fully protected and secured.

...and other emergency services.

'Mountain rescue teams are called out through the police via the 999 system.'

'As you say, sir... the Chief Constable will most definitely be hearing about this.'

'What was that you were saying about cultivating good relationships with the statutory services?'

It's not uncommon for boundary lines to become a contentious issue between neighbours.

Mountain and cave
rescue teams frequently
work very closely
together on incidents.

You will be involved in a wide variety of incidents...

...often operating in extremely difficult situations in regard to weather and terrain.

Once on a call out,
mountain rescuers are,
to a person, single
minded and focused on
the job in hand.

'Besides poor visibility, deteriorating weather conditions, cold, wet and fatigue, being lost quickly conjures up all sorts of emotions – fear loneliness, depression, apprehension, anger, embarrassment. In fact, being lost in itself isn't really the problem. The problem is the fear of what might happen next.'

'You've been reported overdue.'

'I see no mountains...'

'A sweep search is effective where there is a high probability that the target is within a known area and may comprise as few as two or three people, with ten or twelve the optimum.'

A daytime sweep is often managed using a system of hand signals.

'Another approach – Purposeful Wandering – is a variation on the traditional theme of team members walking the line abreast and shows a very high detection rate over rough ground. In this instance, searchers use their initiative to check out all the likely spots within the area themselves.'

'So... in a nutshell... wander up the hill and, with a bit of luck, you'll bump into them...'

Their border disputes temporarily put to one side, neighbouring teams will often work together on incidents.

...with navigation and route planning key to the success of a search.

'...past the church and the pub and you'll see the mountains on your left...'

'Key areas of weakness in people's skills are map reading and navigation, especially in adverse or winter conditions when you can't see your destination.'

'Are you sure we can trust this new fangled computerised route plotter gizmo?'

'Mobile Two from Searchie Four... I know we talked about hedging our bets but this is ridiculous... over.'

'Around one third of reported mountain accidents are down to poor navigation. It's not uncommon for people to go for a walk up a hill, confident of their own safety, only to become extremely disorientated by a sudden change...'

'Just like the back of your hand, eh?'

'...there's a man... he
needs your help... he's
on a hill... it's green,
very green...'

'I think it's a grid reference...'

And things don't always go entirely to plan.

Mountain rescue in the UK is provided free of charge to the casualty.

Some teams have skills in water rescue.

'When the TL suggested we train in water rescue this wasn't quite what I had in mind.'

Always take advantage
of stepping stones to
cross a river...

'Risk assessment?
Of course I did a risk
assessment.'

Teams approach water
rescue in different ways.

Animal rescues are not uncommon.

'Trust me...
I'm a vegetarian.'

'So there's no truth in
the old red rag to a bull
myth then?'

'He says he wants to be rescued by the Fire Service.'

And finally...

When team members move to a different part of the
country, whether for work or family reasons, they will
often maintain their mountain rescue involvement by
applying to join the local team in the area – and might
well be required to undergo a period of probation with
their new team.

We've had an attractive offer for you from a less busy team.'

Incident patterns are
by no means seasonal,
so between call outs
you will be able to get
out on the hill....